Napoleon

ANTHONY MASTERS

Longman

1. Immortality

On a December day in 1840, a hundred thousand people lined the streets of Paris in freezing temperatures to watch an extraordinary procession. The body of a man, dead and buried for nineteen years, had been dug up again and laid inside a hearse in the form of a Greek temple nine metres high. This was dragged by sixteen black horses in an agonizingly slow procession through what had once been his capital city. The great church of the Invalides, brilliantly lit by massive chandeliers and hung with black drapes, was packed with six thousand shivering VIPs, including the King, Louis Philippe, and Queen Marie-Amélie.

The man they honoured was Napoleon. Louis-Philippe, in particular, must have watched the scene with mixed feelings. His family, the Bourbons, had ruled France since the 16th century. They had been exiled while he was still a boy. His cousin, Louis XVI, had had his head cut off by men whose professed aim was to abolish tyranny. Barely ten years later, Napoleon had come to power. Even in his lifetime, his name had become synonymous with tyranny.

Yet the devotion Napoleon still inspired was incredible. Survivors of his Imperial Guard, the crack force he had led to victory so many times, followed his body in the bitter cold, 25 years after he had been taken from them into exile. When his original grave on St. Helena was opened and the coffin lid removed, the Emperor's former attendants, who had travelled two months by sea to bring him home, wept openly to see their master, uncannily preserved and still very nearly lifelike. To those of his subjects who had lived through his coronation and seen him return as the victorious hero, he was like a god. It is said that old people in the

Cyr École Polytechnique.   Garde Nationale à cheval.   Un Lieutenant Général et son État Major.   Cheval de Bataille.   Commission de St. Hélène.   B.

Napoleon's Europe

LONGMAN GROUP LIMITED
Longman House
Burnt Mill, Harlow, Essex, UK

Produced by Cameron & Tayleur (Books) Ltd.,
25 Lloyd Baker Street, London WC1X 9AT

First published 1981

Printed in Belgium
by Fabrieken Brepols n.v, Turnhout
Setting by Input Typesetting Ltd., London
Reproduction by Brian Gregory Associates Ltd,
St Albans, Herts

Series editors: Ian Cameron, Jill Hollis
Designed by Ian Cameron

British Library Cataloguing in Publication Data

Masters, Anthony
  Napoleon.—(Longman great lives; 4).
  1. Napoleon 1, *Emperor of the French*—Juvenile
  literature
  2. France—Kings and rulers—|Biography
  —Juvenile literature
  I. Title
  944.05'092'4   DC203
  ISBN 0-582-39040-0

Frontispiece: an
unfinished portrait of
Napoleon by Jacques-
Louis David.

Picture credits
Photo Bulloz: 8a; 36b; 43a; 47; 64; 65
Brown University: 57
Cooper-Bridgeman Library: 5; 41; 44
Michael Holford Library: 45; 59
Lauros-Giraudon: 7; 11; 13; 14; 17; 19; 23; 25a, b;
  37; 38; 46a; 49; 52; 55b; 56; 62; 63; 66
Philippa Lewis: 8b; 21a, b; 28a, b; 33
The Longman Group: 15b; 18; 35
Louvre, Paris: 5; 18; 29
The Mansell Collection: 6; 7; 15a; 16a; 32; 34a; 36a;
  50; 54; 61
Musée Condé, Chantilly: 19; 25a
Musée de l'Armée, Paris: 52; 56
Musée Légion d'Honneur, Paris: 66
Musée Nationale du Château de Malmaison: 17; 43a;
  46c
Musée Nationale du Château de Versailles: 8a; 23; 37;
  43b; 65
National Army Museum, London: 60
National Gallery of Art, Washington: 41
National Portrait Gallery, London: 34b
Picturepoint, London: 29; 31; 43b; 55a; 57
Prado, Madrid: 44
Tate Gallery, London: 35
Weidenfeld & Nicolson Archives: 9; 10; 12; 166; 21c;
  27; 42; 46b, c, d; 51
Wellington Museum, London: 45; 55a; 59

Map by Creative Cartography Ltd. (Terry Allen and
  Nicholas Skelton).

Contents

Napoleon's body is exhumed on St. Helena nineteen years after his death. A 19th-century illustration.

Napoleon's funeral procession in Paris in 1840. *Below:* the hearse followed by survivors of the Old Guard, the Emperor's personal troops. *Left:* the head of the procession approaching the Church of the Invalides.

country walked many kilometres to the banks of the Seine, just to see the boat that carried his coffin back to Paris.

The great novelist Stendhal, who actually worked under him, wrote that "my love for Napoleon is the only passion remaining to me," adding that his "extraordinary talents ... made him the most amazing human being to appear since Caesar..." Most people who met Napoleon were impressed by the force and concentration of his glance, the power of his speech and writing, his ceaseless energy and, when he chose, the charm of his smile. His magic still persists; writers have praised his genius as a general, as a lawyer, as an administrator, even (improbably) as an idealistic social reformer.

Yet Napoleon also had his critics. Madame de Staël, a leading writer and conversationalist who knew him, maintained that he regarded virtue, dignity of feeling and religion

l'Empereur.   Quatre quadriges maintenus par des Ecuyers à la livrée de l'Empereur.   **Char Funèbre.** Quatre Maréchaux tenant les Cordons.   Marins de la Belle-Poule.   Vieille Garde.

7

The writer Madame de Staël (*above*) was not one of the Emperor's admirers, but few famous men can have been the subject of as much adulatory literature as Napoleon. *Right:* an illustration by "Job" from a 1910 biography, *Bonaparte* by G. Montorgeuil. It shows the young Napoleon working by candlelight at the Royal Military School in Brienne; the shadow on the wall is that of Napoleon as Emperor.

as "enemies of the continent". For the contemporary Press and public in Britain, threatened for a while with French invasion, he became "Boney" – a bogey-man to frighten naughty children, a monster of "fraud and hypocrisy, and blasphemy, and impiety, and cruelty and injustice." In France, nobody could dare say such a thing while he was alive. His secret police saw to that. Even after his death, French scholars editing his letters cut out some of his more brutal paragraphs on the grounds that they were "illegible".

Many people who had at first admired him changed their minds as they saw him becoming a dictator. Beethoven, who had dedicated his Eroica symphony to Napoleon, ripped out the page in disgust, on hearing that his hero had crowned himself Emperor, and bitterly rewrote the dedication, "To the memory of a great man."

Who was this man who inspired his people to so many triumphs and aroused such conflicting passions?

The little Corsican

Napoleone Buonaparte was born at Ajaccio in Corsica on 15th August 1769. At that time, Corsica and its inhabitants had a reputation for roughness. Life there was far from peaceful. Up to 1761, the Italian State of Genoa had had

8

the difficult task of governing the island with what seemed to be the entire Corsican population engaged in guerrilla warfare against the foreign oppressors. When the Genoese were at last expelled, the respite was brief. A few months before Napoleon was born, the French arrived, crushed the Corsican resistance and took over. After that, Corsica was French, and consequently Napoleon was a French citizen.

Carlo Buonaparte, Napoleon's father, had been a resistance leader, but he quickly submitted to the French and was recognized as a member of the French nobility. They spoke Italian – it was Corsica's language – and sounded the "e" at the end of their surname. (Later, Napoleon discreetly spelt it in a more French way as Bonaparte and pronounced it as only three syllables.)

Carlo and his wife, Letizia, had married for love when they were very young: he was 18, she was 14. Carlo was handsome, charming, intelligent and an appalling spendthrift. He is said to have spent two years' income on a single party. He wrote well in prose and verse, and, when short of money, proved himself extremely resourceful and tactful at

Napoleon's mother, Letizia Buonaparte (1750–1836).

dealing with people. He died in his late thirties in 1785, when Napoleon was only sixteen. Letizia, on the other hand, died in her mid-eighties and outlived even her famous son. She had an iron constitution and a very strong personality. Once, when the teenage Napoleon had displeased her, she was cunning enough to wait until he was changing for dinner before marching into his bedroom with her cane. When he was Emperor and tried to make her kiss his hand in homage, her fan came down on his knuckles very smartly indeed. At the height of his and his brothers' power, she refused to spend a penny more than necessary, saying, "I may one day have to find bread for all these kings I have borne."

Carlo and Letizia had eleven children, eight of whom reached adulthood. Napoleon was only the second of the eight, but he was always the dominant child of the family. There is one story that he was born with a great roar, as if announcing to the world that he had arrived to take it over, and another that, less than two years later, when he was being baptized, he distinctly said to the priest, "Don't wet me!"

Napoleon had the knack of getting his own way. "I had the instinct," he said later, "that my willpower was stronger than other people's. I had to get anything I wanted." When his class at school was split into two teams, the Romans and the Carthaginians, Napoleon refused to be a Carthaginian,

Napoleon in command
of a snowball fight at
Brienne.

knowing that they had been the losers. So his elder brother Joseph, who was a Roman, had to change places with him. At other times, we are told, he used to bite and beat Joseph, and then run to his mother and complain that he was being bullied. However, when the two brothers were finally sent to separate schools at the age of nine or ten, both of them wept. Joseph wept profusely. Napoleon shed only one tear, but the schoolmaster who was present said it expressed just as much.

Napoleon's new school was the Royal Military School at Brienne in Champagne, in the northern part of France. The teachers, who were monks, were generally easygoing and not particularly academic. The living conditions, however, were very strict: a good training for a man who was to declare, "Poverty and misery make a soldier." Even in the depths of winter the boys were allowed only one blanket on their camp-beds.

Napoleon shone at mathematics, geography and history. History remained his passion throughout his life. When he was Emperor, he still read early medieval history for pleasure. His spelling remained very shaky, which later brought disapproval from those secretaries who could actually decipher his atrocious handwriting. He was very homesick at Brienne. He did not mix with the other boys, who picked on him because of his Corsican origins, and he preferred to spend most of his spare time working hard in a little garden he had made himself in the school grounds. Sometimes he would just sit there reading, or thinking, determined to maintain his solitude and furious when he was disturbed. Forty years later, when exiled on St. Helena at the very end of his life, he took up gardening again, finding that it both relieved his boredom and soothed his nerves.

Jean-Pierre Blanchard is sighted between Calais and Boulogne on the north coast of France in January 1785 after making the first sea crossing by balloon, across the English Channel from Dover.

There are stories of his daring, which must have impressed even his hostile schoolmates. When the great aeronaut Jean-Pierre Blanchard made one of his first balloon ascents, the intrepid young Napoleon got himself into the newspapers by trying to break through the barriers and get into the basket with him. In the bitter winter of 1783, he had his first experience of generalship, building snow forts and ramparts in the school yard and organizing pitched battles. Characteristically, he managed to direct both "armies" simultaneously.

At the age of fifteen, he was awarded a place at France's main military academy, the École Militaire in Paris, where in one year he completed a course that took most students two or three. Here, he really came up against snobbery. Many of his fellow-students were aristocrats, only too ready to mock his unfashionable clothes or his Corsican accent. Legend has it that, on winter nights, they would stand in a line before the fire, to stop him from warming himself. Many of them had no intention of pursuing military careers. Their parents had sent them to the École Militaire because of its prestigious riding school, as riding was a necessary accomplishment for a gentleman. The students who did aim at a commission relied on their fathers' influence and knew there was no point in working hard.

Napoleon had no such advantages, but he did well at the school. He had been there only four months when his father died on 24th February 1785. It had been known for some time that he was suffering from incurable stomach cancer. On his deathbed, Carlo Buonaparte called repeatedly for Napoleon. "Where is Napoleon, my son Napoleon, whose sword will make kings tremble and who will change the face of the world?"

2. Revolution

Napoleon's unique value in his father's eyes is easy to explain. As he grew up, he developed from a moody and aggressive child into a mature and responsible young man. When he was not quite fifteen, he was already writing in a masterful tone to his uncle about the progress and career of his brothers, older as well as younger: "Joseph," he wrote maturely, "could do best of the whole family if he worked. Now he wants to enter the Services – a decision in which he is very much mistaken." He goes on to say why: Joseph was not very strong and would only make a good garrison officer who would get on well in society. His father's death increased the confidence and sense of responsibility that were naturally part of Napoleon's character.

Graduating from military school at the age of sixteen, Napoleon was ready for the life of an officer, starting as a second lieutenant in an artillery regiment stationed at Valence. A drawing made by a friend, now in the museum at Versailles, captures his appearance at the time. He had fine, straight hair hanging to below the collar, a noble profile, a finely moulded nose and bright, intent eyes. Napoleon's increasing command of military arts brought him regular promotion, but his intellectual interests and dogmatic attitudes made him unpopular with his colleagues.

When he was alone, he suffered great depression. Separated from his homeland, he became almost suicidal with frustration as he brooded on his incapacity to free Corsica. Fortunately, his romantic streak could bring him idyllic happiness as well as anguish. He fell in love with the daughter of his landlady at Valence, and, as he wistfully recalled at the end of his life, spent innocently blissful mornings just eating cherries with her and gazing into her eyes.

He read and wrote ceaselessly, particularly about history. He believed that kingship, as such, is just a historical accident. "There are only a very few kings" he wrote in October 1788, "who do not deserve to lose their thrones." A few months later, the events were set in motion that were to overthrow the monarchy.

At this time, every aspect of French life was still dominated by the aristocracy. Members of noble families took the key positions in the Government, the Army and the Church. In theory, France was ruled by an absolute monarch, but Louis was short of money, and his authority was weak.

Napoleon as a military cadet at the age of sixteen in 1785. This sketch by a friend is the earliest known picture of him.

The middle classes in the cities and even some of the nobility were adopting the ideas of freedom that had been expressed by French writers such as Voltaire and Jean-Jacques Rousseau. But the vast majority of Frenchmen were peasants working on the land and often exploited for rents, taxes and cheap labour by the local noblemen. In 1789, the peasants in many parts of France rebelled against the aristocracy in a wave of violence called the Great Fear.

The first stages of the revolution did not put an end to the monarchy, but the feudal privileges of the aristocracy were abolished and the government was taken over by a National Assembly. In 1791, the King tried to escape from France with his family.

Safely abroad, he would be able to count on the support of other European monarchs, who feared that their own positions would be threatened if the fashion for revolution spread. The Queen, Marie-Antoinette, was herself an Austrian, and France's neighbours harboured many *émigrés*— aristocrats who had already fled the country. But the Royal Family were stopped before they reached the border, and France declared war on Austria in April 1792.

Napoleon played no active role in the French Revolution. A succession of postings in various parts of France kept him away from the scene of action. He was in Paris briefly in the summer of 1792. When an armed mob invaded the Tuileries, he was there, voicing his disapproval of the chaotic scene and saying that if he were King, such things would

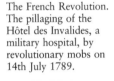

The French Revolution. The pillaging of the Hôtel des Invalides, a military hospital, by revolutionary mobs on 14th July 1789.

MORT DE LOUIS CAPET NOM LE 21 JANVIER 1793.

A contemporary engraving of the execution of Louis XVI at the guillotine. In true revolutionary style, the title of the picture does not allow him his royal title. It reads: "Death of Louis Capet, sixteenth of that name, 21st January 1793."

not be tolerated. The King's execution in 1793, and the bloodbath that followed, again found him an eager spectator from afar. By March 1793, France was at war with Prussia, Austria, Britain and Holland.

In this war, promotion for talented men was rapid. The army was desperately short of officers, since many of them had been aristocrats who had died at the guillotine in the Revolution or had fled abroad. At the age of 24, Napoleon, as Captain-Commandant under the incompetent General Carteaux, was dispatched to the south of France. Lyons, Marseilles and Avignon were all in revolt against the revolutionary government in Paris. Worst of all, the revolt had spread to France's great naval base, Toulon, on the Mediterranean coast. On 23rd August 1793, Toulon surrendered to the British together with the entire French Mediterranean fleet.

Toulon was guarded by the British fleet, stretched out in the harbour below the fort of L'Eguillette which was occupied by the British. Early on in the siege, the French artillery commander was severely wounded; Napoleon was on the spot (initially, it seems to have been just a social call), and was appointed to the job. It was the sort of luck that seems reserved for really great men. The French government troops had only to set up a battery there to have the British fleet at

Paul-François Barras, an aristocrat from Provence in southern France who had supported the Revolutionary side and became one of the country's Directors.

The siege of Toulon, 19th December 1793. Flying from the ramparts is the *tricolor* flag of Revolutionary France; at the head of the flagpole is the *bonnet rouge*, the red cap of liberty.

their mercy. Taking no heed of General Carteaux's reservations, Napoleon took the initiative, ruthlessly ensuring that he got the necessary guns, and the men to fire them. Carteaux was angry, but his wife calmed him by observing that he, Carteaux, would get the credit if Napoleon succeeded, but that only Napoleon would lose face if he failed.

Napoleon had first to dislodge the British from L'Eguillette to gain his commanding position. He had to set up no fewer than eight gun batteries to bombard the British fort before they would abandon it. One battery was in such an exposed position that none of Napoleon's troops would man it, thinking it certain suicide. Napoleon put up a notice which read, "This is the battery of men who know no fear." It was always manned after that.

Immediately after the evacuation of L'Eguillette, the British admirals saw that their cause was lost and abandoned Toulon. Napoleon proudly wrote back to his superiors in Paris, but he did not receive much credit for his deed. Most of the official glory went to Paul-François Barras, the high government official sent to report on the situation, but in return Napoleon was to find Barras a very useful ally.

One minister who did recognize Napoleon's merits was Augustin Robespierre, brother of the great Revolutionary leader, Maximilien Robespierre but within a few months Napoleon found that this was a dangerous friendship. In the summer of 1794 the political situation changed, and both the Robespierres were executed. Napoleon was arrested on suspicion of treason, because of his friendship with the Robespierres. He spent an anxious fortnight in prison wondering what his fate would be. Had he been in Paris, he

BONAPARTE
Général en Chef de l'Armée d'Italie.

[handwritten letter]

Maximilien Robespierre, one of the most prominent leaders of the French Revolution. The execution of Robespierre and his followers on 28th July 1794 brought an end to the terror, in which many thousands of people were guillotined. This sketch is by the famous painter Jacques-Louis David.

would have been guillotined at once, but he was arrested some distance away, and this gave his influential friends time to secure his release.

During the last months of the Revolution, the political scene changed constantly. In 1795, the Revolutionary government was finally replaced by a ruling committee of five self-elected Directors. This marked the end of the terror and peace returned to Paris. Under the patronage of Barras, who was a Director and one of France's most influential men, Napoleon entered elegant society.

Josephine

Three months later he met a beautiful widow of thirty-two, Josephine de Beauharnais. She was a Creole, born in Martinique, a dusky-skinned beauty of faintly exotic appearance, not educated but clever and stylish, and immensely fascinating. Her husband had been sentenced to death during the Revolution, and she had got herself arrested trying to save him. He was executed, and she only escaped the same fate through illness. When she recovered, she found herself reprieved, and a widow. Soon afterwards, it was Napoleon's job to collect all weapons from private houses in the district where she lived. She had to give up her husband's sword, but sent her teenage son, Eugène, to plead for its return as a treasured relic. Napoleon was touched and granted the request. In due course, Josephine went personally to thank him. After a brief, torrid flirtation, they were married. Unusually, she was six years older than he – a fact that she concealed on the marriage certificate.

He was wildly in love with her. However, Josephine's initial fascination with Napoleon must have worn off at an early stage. Within a couple of years, her affairs were the talk of Paris, and the relationship soon became very stormy indeed. At times his treatment of her was little short of barbarous, as in the notorious incident when he forced her to drive her carriage across a dangerous gully, even when he knew she was frightened to death. But all this was in the future. The war with the other European countries was still going on, and, a few days after Napoleon's marriage in March 1796, renewed hostilities against the Austrians and Sardinians in Italy snatched him away, and he wrote passionate love-letters to Josephine: "You have robbed me of more than my heart: you are the only thought I have . . . I feel passion strangling me. The day when I lose your heart, Nature will lose for me all her warmth and greenery. . . ". We must not forget this spontaneity and love even though, in later years, he used and discarded a number of women without any emotion, and, after little more than ten years, divorced Josephine herself.

Left: part of one of the passionate though illegible letters written to Josephine by Napoleon in Italy.

Italy

Napoleon's performance as a general remained superbly professional. At first, the other commanders mistrusted his youth and found his puny appearance unimpressive, but "he spoke with such dignity, preciseness and competence that his generals retired with the conviction that at last they had a real leader."

Already, at this early stage of his career, he had grasped one of the essential facts of generalship: that battles are

Josephine as Empress, painted by François Gérard.

A heroic portrait by Antoine-Jean Gros of Napoleon leading his soldiers across the bridge at Arcola in northern Italy in November 1796, six months after his triumph at the battle of Lodi.

often won simply because the victor organizes his forces so that they can be rapidly assembled in overwhelming numbers. The secret was partly skilful placing, but Napoleon also trained his troops to cover long distances at great speed. In one battle of the 1796 campaign in Italy, he managed to gather together 25,000 men, nearly half of whom had to march 24 kilometres uphill to reach their target. He ordered his troops to attack frontally, while he diverted the enemy's attention by a surprise attack on the flank.

The Italian campaign was swift, an almost unbroken line of successes. In Milan, Napoleon was received as a liberator, the inhabitants actually scattering flowers in his path. After only six weeks, he negotiated his own treaty with Sardinia, driving an exceedingly hard bargain. Again, he did his best to ensure that his efforts were appreciated at home. The battle of Lodi, when the French managed to force their way across the town's bridge under heavy fire, passed into popular legend as a stupendous piece of personal bravery by

Napoleon himself, waving his sword and urging on his men regardless of danger. He later said, "It was not till that evening that I knew I was superior to other men, and actually planned to put into practice the great ideas that, till then, had filled my thoughts only as a fantastic dream." By the end of the campaign, Napoleon was effectively the ruler of Italy, and the Austrian Archduke was forced to sue for peace. Napoleon was beginning to acquire a position of unique power as a disposer of the fate of nations. In fact, his personal success gave him a reputation on the political as well as on the military scene and brought him considerably closer to power. Joined at last by Josephine, he occupied the palace of the Crevellis just outside Milan, where he established a semi-royal court and even ate his dinner in full view of the public, just as Louis XIV had done. He went on to conquer Venice. When he returned to Paris at the end of 1797, he received a hero's welcome. The government, eager to honour him, presented him with a vast lump sum and a pension.

While he was still in Italy, Napoleon had received a letter from Charles-Maurice de Talleyrand, who was now Foreign

Charles-Maurice de Talleyrand, who had been Bishop of Autun before the Revolution. As French Foreign Minister under the Directory, he supported Napoleon in his rise to power.

Minister, complimenting him and pledging his support. They were to remain very closely associated for the next ten years. Talleyrand was fifteen years older, an experienced diplomat and a very shrewd judge of character. Having served under Louis XVI, he was forced to flee first to England and then to America during the Revolution. He returned to France when the Directory had been established and later held office under Napoleon and under Louis XVIII, after Napoleon had been deposed. He remained constantly in favour because of his great discretion and diplomacy, and ended his public life as French Ambassador in London in 1834, when he was eighty.

Egypt

It was Talleyrand, in fact, who first officially introduced Napoleon to the Directors, and he also gave a magnificent party in honour of Josephine. Though his success in Italy was flattering to his self-esteem, Napoleon was well aware that his prestige would need to be carefully maintained. "In Paris, nothing is remembered for long," he wrote. Something more glorious, more superb still, was needed to fix him in the public imagination. He decided on an expedition to Egypt, very probably at Talleyrand's suggestion. Egypt would be a rich prize: it could provide a gateway to India, which France had been compelled to give almost entirely to the British a generation earlier. Egypt also held a unique position on the world's trade-routes. Occupying it would be a blow against Britain.

Napoleon sketched after the battle of Lodi in 1796.

Napoleon was given a free hand in organizing the expedition. It was to be both a military and scholarly enterprise as Napoleon had an intellectual interest in exploring Egypt as well as wanting to seize it for strategic reasons. So, to the surprise of many Frenchmen, a whole corps of scientists, architects, archaeologists and academics accompanied the expeditionary force that set sail for Egypt on 19th May 1798.

Landing on 2nd July, Napoleon quickly captured Alexandria, and then pressed on across the desert to Cairo. This was not one of the best organized or most glorious episodes in Napoleon's career. The army marched under scorching sun, generally without food or water and frequently under attack. Many men died from their ordeal; some even committed suicide. Boots and clothing fell to pieces. Eventually, what was left of the army reached the Pyramids, where they were faced by a considerable force of Egypt's military class, the Mamelukes. Though they were near exhaustion, the

Above: Napoleon, as General in command of the armed forces in France, facing the hungry mob in Les Halles, the market area of Paris. *Right:* Napoleon, evading the British fleet, sails back to France from Egypt on a fast and heavily armed frigate. Even so, the voyage took almost seven weeks. Two illustrations by "Job".

French won the battle decisively. The Mamelukes were massacred, and Napoleon's troops went on to take Cairo without resistance.

In Cairo, Napoleon had his first opportunity of proving himself as lawgiver and administrator. His enlightened and efficient rule in Cairo gave the world a foretaste of what was to follow. He surveyed the country, built hospitals and military cemeteries. The expeditions' scholars were able to research Egypt's past and open up the field of Egyptian studies. They found and deciphered the Rosetta Stone, making it possible for scholars to read other Egyptian inscriptions. The French also introduced Egypt to the many influences of Western Europe. Napoleon was not only a conqueror. In the Egyptian enterprise, he saw an opportunity to discover and share the magic of a new civilization. In Cairo he published newspapers. (Journalism remained one of his interests, in which he combined his natural talent for crisp, powerful writing with his understanding of the importance of propaganda.)

Shortly after Napoleon reached Cairo, however, the British fleet, commanded by Admiral Nelson, destroyed the French fleet in the Battle of the Nile. As a result, Napoleon was unable to get news of the political situation in Paris. However, his sixth sense told him that political change was imminent in Paris. Leaving a subordinate in charge, he sailed for home.

3. Taking Power

It was the autumn of 1799. There had been an increasing number of problems for the Directory during Napoleon's absence. The war in Italy had flared up again and was going badly, while there were severe financial problems at home. As the Directory's authority was very weak, Talleyrand agreed with Napoleon that it was time to overthrow them. The two of them held regular meetings, sometimes with Napoleon's brother Lucien, who was president of one of the Councils of State, and sometimes with the Abbé Sieyes, the strongest of the Directors and one of Talleyrand's supporters.

The drama that ended the Directory took place at Saint-Cloud, a former royal palace just outside Paris, on 9th and 10th November 1799. The two legislative bodies of France, the Council of Elders and the Council of Five Hundred (of which Lucien Bonaparte was president) were directed to meet at Saint-Cloud, away from the threat of popular demonstrations – but, as Napoleon was quick to realize, the meetings could still be easily disrupted. Most of the Directors were forced to resign, and Napoleon interrupted and harangued the meetings of both Councils. In the Council of Five Hundred, despite Lucien's efforts to keep order, ugly scenes took place, and voices were even heard declaring Napoleon an outlaw. Seeing a show of force as the only solution, the two brothers together won over the Council guards and then marched with them into the hall. The outcome of the action was that the two councils were forced to "elect" Napoleon, Sieyes and a colleague called Ducos as Consuls of the Republic. During the Revolution, France had adopted a new calendar in which each month had a name connected with the seasons. November was Brumaire, the "month of mists". Consequently, Napoleon's take-over became known as the *coup d'état de Brumaire*.

The outcome did not satisfy Napoleon. Weeks of tense bargaining followed, in which he had the upper hand. His determination was invincible, and he had popularity working in his favour. Eventually he secured the position of First Consul; the other two consuls were nominated by him and had no real power. The road to absolute authority now lay wide open, and Napoleon had the chance to bring about major administrative reforms for his native country.

Over the next few years, aided by his immense capacity

Napoleon at the Council of Five Hundred at Saint-Cloud in November 1799.

for work and his ability to terrify subordinates into over-working as much as he did, he proceeded to reorganize the government, laws and educational system of France. There was hardly an aspect of French life that escaped being examined and regulated; his efforts extended to such things as funeral prices, gambling, forestry and the distribution of theatres in Paris. In all this, he showed himself to be one of the world's greatest administrators.

Napoleon believed that efficient government, in particular the efficient collection of taxes, depended on control from the centre, and in this case the centre was himself. By an Act passed in February 1800, France was divided into 98 *départements*, each controlled by an official called a *préfet*, and this system of government still exists in modern France. Napoleon appointed all but the most junior officials, and they were personally answerable to him. Napoleon's government machine was ruthlessly efficient. It made its own contribution to the feeling of national unity and patriotism

23

that Napoleon hoped would lead France (and himself) to glory.

Another area in which Napoleon's reforms benefit France even now is that of the law. The *Code Napoléon*, originally called the *Code Civil*, was complete and systematic to a degree unknown in previous history. As Napoleon himself was a clear, concise writer, he had the old-fashioned statute books used by lawyers rewritten in language that could be understood by everyone. Napoleon often attended meetings of the committee that compiled the Code, and, we are told, could surpass the cleverest men present in getting to the heart of a question, through the force of his arguments and the originality of his expressions.

Education remained one of Napoleon's particular interests throughout his life. Though he loathed intellectual women and had no intention of letting girls learn languages, philosophy or anything that would encourage them to think for themselves, he believed that both girls and boys should recognize their responsibilities to the nation. His concern was not essentially for the welfare of his young citizens, but for the State: the State needed administrators, civil servants, officers in the army and navy, and loyal wives and mothers. Boys under twelve, he wrote in 1801, should learn not only mathematics, Latin, drawing, dancing, reading, writing, grammar and the use of arms, but "the elements of ancient history." After the age of twelve, they were given either a "civil education," including Latin and Greek, rhetoric, philosophy, and some mathematics, or a military one, which included advanced mathematics and astronomy as well as the practical skills of war. As for the girls, Napoleon once said, "I do not think we need bother about the education of young girls . . . Marriage is their destination."

In 1808, Napoleon established the University. It was not so much a university in the usual sense as a board in control of education, laying down the curriculum, even the time-table, which became standardized over the whole of France. The teachers had to swear allegiance to the University's laws. They were not allowed to marry until they had "proved" their capacity to maintain themselves and their family, in fact until the age of 25 or 30. In any case, under the *Code Napoléon*, men under 26 and women under 21 could not marry without their parents' consent; up to 30 and 25 respectively, they still had to ask for this, once a month for three months before the wedding. Napoleon himself, it will be remembered, married at 26 precisely.

The First Consul took good care to maintain his popularity. Napoleon's natural glamour was enhanced by Josephine's beauty and social grace; he never had cause to dread unpopularity among the mass of the people. Intellectuals were a different matter. He always hated and feared intelligent men with a political consciousness, and took care to keep them as controlled and as ill-informed as possible. An active secret police, administered by his henchman Fouché, exercised the control, while official newspapers, coupled with ruthless censorship of unofficial publications, took care of the information. (Napoleon wrote a number of leading articles in the government newspaper, the *Moniteur*, himself.) Books and plays were also censored, and their texts were scanned for any line that might seem to encourage anti-Napoleonic sentiments.

In August 1802, supporters of Napoleon pressed the Senate to propose that all three Consuls should hold office for life. Napoleon, though, was in no hurry to seize ultimate power. The right moment came two years later; and, ironically enough, it was his enemies who provided it.

In 1804, a group of men who wanted to return a Bourbon king to government, plotted a take-over, which may well have included a plan to assassinate Napoleon. Betrayed by an informer, the ring-leaders were arrested. Although it was believed that one of the Bourbon princes was involved,

Napoleon painted as First Consul in 1803 by François Gérard. *Right:* Joseph Fouché who ran Napoleon's secret police.

no-one knew which. Although the Comte d'Artois (who, in 1824, after Napoleon's death, was to ascend the French throne as King Charles X) was the most plausible suspect, he could not be caught. Instead, Fouché's police crossed the border into Baden, on the Rhine, a foreign state, where the young Duc d'Enghien was quietly living in exile. They arrested him and took him back to France for trial.

The Duc d'Enghien was definitely innocent. Nevertheless, Napoleon was determined to have him executed. Enghien was taken from his prison in the middle of the night, given a perfunctory trial and executed by firing squad barely an hour later. Napoleon refused to see him.

Enghien's execution was one of the most widely criticized acts of his career. Napoleon almost certainly knew that this particular Bourbon was innocent and put him to death simply to discourage other attempts to seize the throne. (One aide also recalled that, according to the Corsican code of vendetta, anyone attacked by one member of a family could avenge himself on another.) Napoleon certainly succeeded in preventing further royalist plots, but he reckoned without the effects on public opinion, not only abroad (where the reaction was, predictably, one of horror) but inside France as well. One of his ministers, probably the cynical Talleyrand, remarked of the execution, "It was worse than a crime; it was a blunder." However, Napoleon himself had no regrets. "I respect the decisions of public opinion when they are justly formed; but it has its caprices which we ought to learn to despise."

Coronation

In due course, Napoleon addressed his Council. Obviously, he said, the plots against his life had moved him to serious anxiety about how France could be kept stable in the event of his death. He said that only setting up a hereditary ruling dynasty to rival the Bourbons could prevent a Bourbon counter-revolution. A successor who was merely elected would stand no chance of survival. The hint could not have been more explicit, and it was quickly taken. In May 1804, the Senate issued a decree that Napoleon Bonaparte, hitherto First Consul, was now Emperor of the French, and that the title was hereditary.

The whole episode shows how Napoleon identified France's interests with his own. He really did see himself as the instrument of Fate, destined to make a particular mark on the world. He never referred to the fact that, in practice, his performance as one of France's great heroes brought him

A contemporary woodcut of the execution of the Duc d'Enghien.

undreamed-of eminence, wealth and power. But this had almost certainly been his ambition from the beginning. When Napoleon was only 22, his brother Lucien perceptively wrote of him: "I have always seen in Napoleon a completely personal ambition that overrides his love for the public good... He seems to have a strong leaning towards tyranny. I think that, if he were king... his name would be loathed by posterity and by every good patriot."

Many people found it very strange that another king should rule France, only a decade after the last king's head had been cut off. Napoleon even determined to re-establish the pomp and pageantry of a royal Court for himself and his consort, Josephine. All of the surviving nobility were required to attend, as well as those of Napoleon's family, friends and fellow-generals to whom he had given newly created titles. The old aristocrats did not like it a bit, but Napoleon was determined to be recognized by them. One lady who declined a Court appointment found herself banished. As in a well-disciplined army, he would have no insubordination. When he received the ladies of the Court, he had them lined up and walked past them, as though inspecting a guard of honour. In fact, the young women found it extremely frightening, and one eyewitness related how, as the Emperor proceeded, you could see a blush on their faces and necks keeping pace with him.

A former royal page, quite old by now, was brought back from retirement in the country to teach the correct court procedure to the new aristocracy. Nothing but the cathedral of Notre Dame would do for the imperial coronation, and no one but the Pope himself would do to officiate. In fact,

Above: Napoleon as First Consul overseeing improvements to the city of Paris. *Right:* Napoleon and Josephine planning their coronation with the artist Jean-Baptiste Isabey, who designed the ceremonial. Two illustrations by "Job".

Napoleon would not allow him to do the actual crowning, but he insisted that the Pope be summoned all the way from Rome to lend authority to the occasion. Pius VII was a saintly man of great dignity, but he was in no position to refuse the invitation, as Napoleon had just concluded an agreement with him, the so-called Concordat with Rome, limiting the powers and privileges of the Roman Catholic Church in France. Plucky but astute, and probably realizing that he would suffer a good deal more at Napoleon's hands, he agreed to confine his role to the anointing, while Napoleon, in what was probably the most typical gesture of his life, crowned himself.

The coronation, which took place on 2nd December 1804, was the grandest that gold could buy. It cost almost a million pounds in modern money and was carefully sanctified by the use of some regalia that had belonged to Charlemagne, the founder of the Holy Roman Empire a thousand years before. A number of houses around Notre Dame, together with some historic monuments, were demolished for the occasion. The cathedral itself got a magnificent new set of offertory vessels and vestments. The making of the ceremonial chairs, stools, tables, benches, carpets, hangings, tapestries, candlesticks and all the other paraphernalia presented a massive task for the workers of Paris. The tailors and jewellers did best of all, adorning every figure in the scene with fabulous costliness. Napoleon's grand Imperial

mantle was of purple velvet, embroidered with gold bees, lined and collared with a massive quantity of Russian ermine; underneath was a white silk tunic, embroidered with gold, white silk breeches and stockings. Even his white shoes were embroidered with gold. The Empress's costume, in white silk, edged in gold and topped with a purple velvet mantle, matched the Emperor's. The crown and insignia for the Pope used over three thousand precious stones.

Everything went well. The only moments of anxiety were when both Napoleon and Josephine, weighed down by their mantles, staggered on the steps of the great throne, and when the Bonaparte sisters had to be reminded by the Emperor to move Josephine's train. Napoleon swore, before the world, to maintain the territory of the French Republic, to respect and enforce liberty, and to govern only in accordance with the interests, happiness and glory of the French people. Then came his acclamation as Emperor and a triumphant ride back to the palace of the Tuileries, where the gardens were adorned with special triumphal arches and columns and a galaxy of lights.

As he and his brother Joseph stood before a mirror, just before they left the palace in the morning, Napoleon said "If only our father could see us now. . ." Their mother, of course, though not in Paris for the coronation, was still very much alive. But her only comment on hearing of her son's glory was cold and brief. "So long as it lasts . . ." she said.

4. Empire Building

From his seizure of power as First Consul until his coronation as Emperor, Napoleon spent most of his time in Paris, absorbing himself in the minutest details of government. It was in Paris that George Jackson, a perceptive young Englishman of sixteen, who later became a distinguished diplomat, saw him in 1801. "I was much struck," he wrote, "by the personal appearance of Bonaparte. Though of low stature – perhaps 5 feet 5 or 6 – his figure is well proportioned, his features are handsome, complexion rather sallow, hair very dark, cut short, and without powder. He has fine eyes, full of spirit and intelligence, a firm, severe mouth, indicating a stern and inflexible will – in a word, you see in his countenance the master mind; in his bearing the man born to rule." The German playwright Kotzebue was equally appreciative: "His profile is that of an ancient Roman – grave, noble, expressive. If he were always silent, this gravity would have something cold in it, and a frightening air of sternness. But the moment he speaks, a kindly smile imparts a gracious line to his mouth, and inspires confidence."

It also inspired confidence in his army. While he tended to be brutal and condescending towards his ministers and executives, believing that their ambition gave them all the encouragement they needed, he never missed an opportunity to raise the morale of his fighting men. In fact, he was an excellent actor. If he wished to be charming, nobody could do it better. He would lick anybody's boots, anybody's, if it suited *his* purpose and furthered *his* power. At other times, his performance took the form of overpowering rage. In reality, however wild his behaviour seemed, Napoleon was very much in control of what he was doing and the effect it would produce. As the wife of one of his aides remarked, "If his ends are served, he does not care what becomes of other people."

His charm worked best, and permanently, on his soldiers. He never thought it beneath him to chat with them, and his presence in battle was a constant inspiration to them. During the appalling retreat of the French from Moscow in 1812, when the cold killed thousands upon thousands of men, soldiers would give the imperial aides some sticks from their campfires, saying, "These are for the Emperor." Three years later, during his brief return to France following his escape from exile in Elba, a detachment was sent to oppose him;

but he recognized in it one of his own veterans, a man with big whiskers. Fixing him in his gaze, the Emperor said "Old Moustache, you were with me at Marengo." Old Moustache admitted it was true, and could not lift a finger against him; nor could his colleagues. It was his power of personality, as well as his formidable brain, that made Napoleon such an extraordinary man.

As First Consul, he had crossed the Alps in 1800 to follow his general and War Minister, Louis Alexandre Berthier, into Italy, where the Austrians had fought back with some success during the closing months of the Directory. On 14th June, he defeated the Austrians at Marengo. It became one of his most famous victories, for which he claimed much personal glory. Shortly afterwards an armistice was signed on terms very favorable to France. The name of Marengo survived, not only as the name of Napoleon's favorite white horse, but also in the title of a famous dish. "Chicken Marengo" – fried chicken and tomatoes braised together in white wine – was the supper improvised by Napoleon's cook from whatever he could get on the spot. Steamed crayfish, presumably caught in the nearby river, completed the concoction.

The battle of Marengo, near Genoa in Italy, at which Napoleon as First Consul won a narrow victory which nevertheless brought him much glory. The painting is by the future General Lejeune.

A brief peace followed, first with Austria, then with Britain but soon both sides were uneasy. The other countries were worried about France's ambitions, and Napoleon was busy extending France's colonies and annexing parts of Italy.

An assortment of French projects for crossing the Channel to invade England: balloons, special boats and a tunnel. The English defences against the balloons appear to be manned kites.

The fighting started again in May 1803, and its second phase was destined to be very different from its first. For one thing, the scenery in which it was fought was totally different: Prussia, Spain and even Russia, instead of northern Italy. This time, too Britain was to play a more important part. The target of a ruthless system of sanctions devised by Napoleon to break the strength of the pound, Britain expected a French invasion. Napoleon's invasion schemes have acquired a certain quaintness with the passing of over a century, but they were all in deadly earnest at the time. Napoleon reckoned he had sympathizers in high places in Britain and was also convinced that the lower classes would welcome him. France had had a revolution and thrown out her ancient monarchy. Why not Britain? Unfortunately, the English working classes were among the most loyal defenders of monarchy. They despised the French for their alleged cowardice and barbarism, and for their refusal to acknowledge that England was, and always would be, superior. There was certainly unrest on the English side of the Channel, generated by hunger and social injustice; but Napoleon, if he had ever landed, would have had a very rude awakening.

Napoleon, though, was confident that he would land and put a great deal of research into how to do it. He made frequent visits to the French Channel ports, remarking once that "The Channel is a mere ditch." He commanded special flat-bottomed boats to be designed but, when the British captured one of the few built, they found them such "wretched vessels . . . contemptible and ridiculous" that they were convinced they were only a blind, and that Napoleon intended his real attack some other way – perhaps by tunnel under the English Channel.

But England was ready too. Faced by the first threat of enemy invasion for 200 years, the country was overwhelmed by a flood of patriotism. Nearly half a million civilians joined the Militia as volunteers, drilling on village greens, on the beaches and in London parks. The rich bought expensive weapons and beautiful made-to-measure uniforms; the poor were issued with pikes, which they rightly felt would not be much use against Bonaparte's artillery. England was able to call on immense reserves of pluck and patriotism. Without much attention to practical details and organization, it was hoped that all would be well on the day.

In the event of a French landing, a chain of beacons would be lit from the coast to carry the news inland. The Court of George III would transfer to Worcester from London, which would naturally be the focus of an enemy attack. On one occasion, the beacons were lit by mistake, drums sounded, and all the volunteers rushed into the streets.

The tension lasted for months. But, as those months wore on, the English became more sceptical about the invasion:

Napoleon watching preparations for the invasion of England. An illustration by "Job".

> This little Boney says he'll come
>   At merry Christmas time,
> But that I say is all a hum,
>   Or I no more will rhyme.
>
> Some say in wooden house he'll glide;
>   Some say in air balloon;
> E'en those who airy schemes deride
>   Agree his coming soon.
>
> Now, honest people, list to me,
>   Though income is but small,
> I'll bet my wig to one pen-ny
>   He does not come at all.

In fact, Napoleon was waiting until his navy was sufficiently in command of the Channel to protect the crossing. That

objective was never achieved; British sea power was the stronger, both in terms of expertise and of actual numbers, while France lost her best naval commander when Admiral Latouche-Tréville suddenly grew ill and died. His successor, Pierre-Charles de Villeneuve, was only appointed because Napoleon believed him to be lucky, like himself. But the "mild and melancholy" Villeneuve was only too conscious that his forces could not achieve what Napoleon expected of them. The plan was to draw the British fleet off to protect the West Indies, splitting it up in the process, before returning quickly to the Channel to cover the invasion.

The French plan was wrecked by Admiral Nelson's defeat of the French at Trafalgar (off the south coast of Spain) in

Admiral Villeneuve, who commanded the French fleet at the battle of Trafalgar.

Admiral Lord Nelson who commanded the British fleet in the battles of the Nile and Trafalgar. He had lost his right arm and his right eye in previous battles.

The Battle of Trafalgar by the great British painter J. M. W. Turner. Nelson is lying at the foot of the main mast of his flagship H.M.S. *Victory*.

1805. Nelson, who led the British fleet, has been a national hero ever since, not only because Trafalgar was a great victory, but because it removed once and for all the threat of a French invasion. Under Nelson's command, the British fleet stuck close together, blockaded Villeneuve and his ships in Cadiz harbour, and, when the French finally emerged, broke their line in two places, throwing it into utter disarray. Nelson himself, strolling the decks of HMS *Victory*, with the Order of the Bath glittering on his breast, was shot by a mast-top marksman. He died just as the British grasped success. Barely a third of the French ships limped back to harbour. Villeneuve, captured at Trafalgar, was returned to France, but killed himself rather than face his master's fury.

Campaigns in Europe

After this, the invasion of England was no longer feasible. Instead, Napoleon concentrated on land operations against Austria and Prussia. Once again, the main points of Napoleonic strategy, concentration of forces and speed of movement, were successful. The Austrians became separated from their Russian allies and, when battle commenced at Ulm in Prussia on 17th October 1805, Napoleon was leading a French force of 200,000 men against 85,000 Austrians. His speed and concentration had brought about a situation

35

where he could not lose. The entire Austrian army was
compelled to surrender.

Six weeks later, at Austerlitz, which was then part of
Austria, he was victorious against the Russians. He concentrated his forces to devastating effect, calling up one corps
of 11,000 men, commanded by the trusted Louis-Nicholas
Davout, all the way from Vienna. Artfully, he positioned
Davout's corps behind two small lakes; when the Russian
centre was defeated, the advancing left wing found itself cut
off. Many Russians were drowned in the freezing waters;
others were captured or slaughtered. Shortly afterwards,
Austria signed a treaty relinquishing her last possession in
Italy, and Russia, too, seemed likely to withdraw from the
conflict. Coming so soon after the news of the victory at
Trafalgar, Austerlitz was a horrible shock to England. The

A contemporary print of
Napoleon at the battle
of Austerlitz, 2nd
December 1805.

36

Marshal Louis-Nicolas Davout whose Third Corps of Napoleon's Grande Armée played an important part in the French victory at Austerlitz.

Prime Minister, William Pitt the Younger, already worn out from being in office almost continuously since ten years before the war started, died a few weeks later, on 23rd January 1806. It was said that Austerlitz had killed him.

Meanwhile, Napoleon moved from success to success. These were his great days, and his army was at its finest, and his strategic brain excelled itself in its ruthless clarity and flexibility. In the following year, 1806, the Prussian Army was practically annihilated at Jena in Saxe-Weimar.

At first, the engagements against the Russians were bloody but indecisive. There was a terrible day in a snowstorm at Eylau, in Lithuania, when one French general wrote after the battle "I have never seen so many dead collected in such a small space. Whole divisions, Russian and French, had been hacked to pieces where they stood. . . . For more than a quarter-league [roughly two kilometres] there was nothing to be seen but heaps of dead. . . ." Finally, at Friedland, on 14th June 1807, seven years to the day after Marengo, Napoleon got the decisive victory he wanted, ending with the hideous slaughter, on the bank of the river Alle, of an entire corps of Russians, who were trapped after the French burned the town bridges.

Russia, too, begged for peace. Napoleon and the Tsar, Alexander I, met to settle the treaty in the bizarre setting of a raft, imperially draped, that was moored in the centre of the river Niemen near Tilsit in Prussia. At the conclusion of each day's talks, they affectionately parted to the accompaniment of trumpets, drums and a gun salute. Alexander was a young man of 29, who greatly admired Napoleon. Their personal relations were cordial throughout. "During the two weeks we spent together," said Napoleon, "we dined together almost every day. We rose early from table so as to be rid of the King of Prussia, who bored us. At nine o'clock, the Tsar, in plain clothes, came to take tea with us. We remained together, talking casually of various subjects, until two or three in the morning." At the time, he wrote to Josephine that he liked the Tsar greatly, and that he had "more intelligence than is commonly thought". In fact, he had more intelligence than even Napoleon thought.

On the face of it, the negotiations went well for Napoleon. In particular, he was able to use Russia against her ally, Britain. The Tsar secretly agreed to try to persuade Britain to make peace with Napoleon too; if the British refused, the Tsar actually promised to declare war.

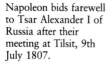

Napoleon bids farewell to Tsar Alexander I of Russia after their meeting at Tilsit, 9th July 1807.

5. Absolute Power

After Tilsit, confident that the conquests were secure, Napoleon returned to his capital to resume the splendours of imperial rule. There were public holidays and pageants and a special service at Notre Dame to celebrate the event.

Napoleon resumed his intense work schedule. Every day he rose at seven and immediately called for a cup of tea or orange-water. Then, perhaps, he would take a bath; he loved bathing and used to spend hours enthroned in his beautiful blue and gold bath with its monograms and imperial symbols. While soaking, he would have the foreign newspapers read to him. He usually did not bother with the French ones, saying, "I already know what's in them." Before dressing, he would have his chest rubbed with a very soft brush, and then massaged with eau de Cologne. Then, the moment he was dressed, work began. He dictated letters in immense quantities, so fast that his secretaries could not keep pace and were obliged to put together afterwards what they thought he would have liked to have said. At nine, he made his first public appearance, saw his ministers and the officers of his household and then proceeded to breakfast, which took only a few minutes. Even dinner, the day's most elaborate meal, was hastily eaten in fifteen or twenty minutes. The French, who take their enjoyment of food so seriously, must have been scandalized.

Then he would go into the Council of State. Sometimes he would be expected; sometimes the drum, beating a salute on the stairs, was an unexpected signal for the councillors to prepare for the worst. He would walk in with his box of snuff in his hand but other snuff-takers would have their boxes instantly confiscated. After helping himself, Napoleon would then lock the boxes away in a drawer. (Cardboard snuffboxes soon became suspiciously common.) He would work his executives extremely hard, keeping meetings going all day with only a quarter of an hour for lunch. Sometimes he would tempt people to give their opinions, then launch "a flood of objections impossible to foresee, still more to combat." One of his great admirers, wrote: "In general, he was very fond of infuriating and disconcerting those who approached him. Sometimes, he pretended not to hear, and made you repeat loudly what he had heard perfectly well (though he was actually a little deaf). At other times, he would overwhelm you with questions so quickly and utterly that you had no time to take them in, and so answered ineptly. Then he drew a lot of enjoyment from your embarrassment, pleased that he had disturbed your presence of mind and self-confidence." Once, at a public reception, he stood in the middle of the room in total silence for ten minutes, until everyone present was almost frantic with apprehension, but the elderly and distinguished Marshal Massena, who eventually tried to help him out, was rudely humiliated.

Ministers found it nerve-racking to serve a man of such unpredictable moods, and the knowledge that Napoleon was often being difficult out of caprice, or sadism, or to feel superior, only made matters worse. He wanted only "yes-men". "To him," as has been said, "discussion seemed insubordination." The result, wrote Stendhal, was, "In 1808 due to the changes which eight years of unhindered arrogance and crown mania had effected in Napoleon's genius, it transpired that, out of his twelve ministers, at least eight were mediocre men having no other merit than that of killing themselves with work. . . ".

Nobody now dared to stop Napoleon from making mistakes. One terrible day, he insisted on having a review of his Boulogne fleet when there was a storm brewing. When an admiral protested, Napoleon flew into a fury and would have struck him with his whip if he had not been prevented. The second-in-command agreed to carry out the order, and more than twenty boats and their crews were lost as a result.

One man who expected the worst was Talleyrand. He believed that the time had come to use his influence and contacts to work for Napoleons's downfall. When the Tsar and Napoleon met for more talks in 1808 at Erfurt in Prussia, Talleyrand had a number of secret interviews with the Tsar, playing on his suspicions of Napoleon and urging him to take a strong line against France. Once back in Paris, his criticisms of the Emperor were outspoken and pungently phrased, in a deliberate attempt to provide his own dismissal.

Retribution was swift. At a special Council meeting, Napoleon began by delivering a general lecture on loyalty, which turned, without the slightest warning, into a full-scale onslaught on Talleyrand. The uncontrolled filthiness of his insults would have left the assembled company speechless if they had not already been too frightened to speak. Talleyrand himself remained totally unruffled, thus accentuating the uncouth impression his master was making. (As he left, he remarked casually, "What a pity that such a great man

Napoleon in his study, a painting by Jacques-Louis David.

should be so ill-bred.") Talleyrand's revenge came later, and in full.

Absolute power was beginning to corrupt Napoleon absolutely. His attitude to people was: "Let them know their master." He thought that, with his secret police, nobody in France dared to be his enemy. He even treated the gentle, saintly Pope like a disloyal subject. When Pius refused to practise economic sanctions against Britain, Napoleon had him arrested in the small hours and dragged across Europe to exile at Savona, near Genoa, in Italy. He remained a prisoner for five years. At one point Napoleon refused him writing materials, books, servants or even a doctor.

Shortly afterwards, there was an attempt on Napoleon's life. In 1809, Austria had recovered herself enough to re-enter the war, but Napoleon once again achieved a quick victory and he entered Vienna. It was there, while Napoleon was inspecting his troops a few days later, that an 18-year-old student, a clergyman's son called Friedrich Staps, was noticed trying to approach him. He was arrested and was found to have a huge kitchen knife in his pocket. In prison, he insisted on speaking to the Emperor. Napoleon had him brought to his study. The boy spoke of his "deep-seated conviction that, by killing you, I should do the greatest service to my country and Europe." Napoleon's shock was intense. It made no sense to him; why try to kill a man whose star had ordained he would bring the whole world to order? Noticing a picture of Stap's girlfriend that had been found on him, Napoleon asked about her reaction. Staps only said, "It will be a great grief to her that I failed. She abhors you as much as I do." Finally, he assured Napoleon that, if he were pardoned, he would make the attempt again. Staps was executed.

The Emperor began to consider the future. He had been wounded in his last campaign. He was worried that he had no successor. He and Josephine had no children, and Josephine was now too old to have any. His brothers, he knew, could not fill his shoes. He must have a son. The only solution was to divorce Josephine.

Though Napoleon's treatment of Josephine had become cold and brutal and though their relationship was quarrelsome and deceitful, he certainly retained some affection for her. The scene when he broke the news to her was dramatic. The Tuileries palace staff heard a scream coming from the

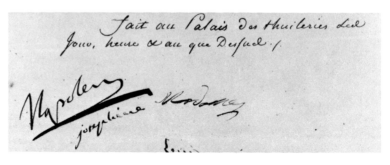

The signatures of Napoleon and Josephine on the transcript of their divorce proceedings.

The marriage of Napoleon and Marie-Louise.

Napoleon's son, the King of Rome, painted in 1815 by Jean-Baptiste Isabey.

salon where the couple had retired after dinner. Rushing in, they found Josephine on the floor, shrieking and moaning. She had to be carried to her room, but outside on the stairs she whispered to a servant supporting her, "You're holding me too tight." Her talent for acting equalled her husband's. For his part, he was genuinely very upset. At the divorce ceremony, a fortnight later, tears were shed by both of them.

His choice of a second wife was ingenious. The Austrian Emperor, whom Napoleon wished to appease following his defeat, had an 18-year-old daughter, Marie-Louise. She was tall – taller than Napoleon – and attractive, but she was very immature and not noticeably intelligent. Napoleon, however, was thrilled with her and took great pains to please her. "Far from treating me badly, as most people believe," she wrote after his death, "he always manifested the deepest regard for me." He had his researchers discover what gifts Louis XVI had provided to welcome Marie-Antoinette, and made sure that Marie-Louise got the same. An entire staff went to meet her. In Vienna, her devoted subjects played French tunes in the streets, rang the church bells and generally gave her an affectionate send-off.

To begin with, Marie-Louise hated the idea. But Napoleon charmed her utterly, as he always did charm people when it was really important. She maintained in later life that she had never cared for him, but in fact, as a very young bride, she had worshipped him. She wrote of her "great happiness", which was only increased when, in March 1811, she gave birth to a son, whom Napoleon made King of Rome. He had his heir at last.

The Peninsular War

Napoleon now involved France in a war in Spain and Portugal, or, as it is usually called, the Peninsular War. The situation in Spain was unstable. The King, Charles IV, was an ageing and weak man. The Queen was having an affair with the Prime Minister, Godoy. The King's son, Ferdinand, hated Godoy, and this made him so popular with the Spanish people that they turned against the King, scaring him into abdicating so that Ferdinand could take his place. But Charles and Godoy were only waiting for their chance to turn the tables.

Napoleon saw an opportunity to secure Spain as a valuable ally in his economic crusade against Britain. Maybe, he

Charles IV and members of his family. Part of a painting by Francisco Goya.

thought, he could even add it to his Empire. So he lured both Charles and Ferdinand across the border to France for separate talks with him, during which Charles was persuaded to resign his claim to the throne to Napoleon, while Ferdinand, unaware of this, resigned his claim in favour of Charles. Napoleon then shut Ferdinand up in one of Talleyrand's country houses and proclaimed his own brother Joseph King of Spain.

Unfortunately, he reckoned without the Spanish people, who were passionately loyal to their prince. There were immediate riots in Madrid, which were suppressed by French troops with terrible savagery. But the spirit of the Spanish was not broken. For the next five years, warfare in Spain was a thorn in Napoleon's flesh. The French army was harassed both by Spanish guerrillas and by British expeditionary forces – the first commanded by Sir John Moore, and the second by Sir Arthur Wellesley, who was soon to become Duke of Wellington.

Arthur Wellesley, First Duke of Wellington, a painting by Sir Thomas Lawrence.

Wellington was very different from Napoleon. He was a meticulous, unflappable man, eminently sensible and fair-minded, hard when necessary, but otherwise tactful and gentlemanly. His officers admired him and trusted his expertise. The campaign was a gruelling one, but Wellington was patient. He took no chances and had the advantage of fighting against French generals who were forced to obey often impractical orders from the Emperor. Through five hard years, Wellington's men kept the French army occupied when it was badly needed by its master in other parts of Europe.

Nevertheless, for the present, Napoleon seemed secure. Austria and Prussia had been brought to heel. The Emperor had his son to succeed him, and his relatives had been given the thrones of the various European countries that he had conquered: Joseph in Naples and Spain, Louis in Holland, and Jérôme in the German state of Westphalia. His general Bernadotte had been declared heir to the throne of Sweden. Eugène de Beauharnais, Josephine's son by her first husband and perhaps the ablest of the whole set, governed Italy as Napoleon's Viceroy. The Emperor's sisters had also done well: Caroline was Queen of Naples, Elise became an Italian Grand-Duchess, and Pauline married an Italian prince and lived in Rome.

But Napoleon was not satisfied. He became convinced that the time had come for war with Russia. This decision had its critics, but many intelligent men believed he was right. In another few years, they argued, Russia might want to extend her territory. Why not strike first, while Napoleon was still there to lead his army?

So strike he did. He went about it in a way that seems utterly typical of his contempt for harsh realities and his blind faith in his own strength, his invincibility, even the good fortune of his "star". "Up there," he would say, pointing to the night sky, "is my star. If you cannot see it, you are a fool and know nothing." His plan was awe-inspiring.

Jean-Baptiste-Jules Bernadotte, a skilled general who was Joseph Bonaparte's brother-in-law. He was elected crown prince of Sweden and adopted by the king, Charles XIII. In 1818, he succeeded his adopted father and reigned as Charles XIV until his death in 1844.

Other Bonapartes. *Left to right:* Elise, Caroline and Joseph.

6. Disaster in Russia

Napoleon decided on a wholesale invasion of Russia with an army of half a million men. "What a man!" said his friend the Count of Narbonne, dazed after an imperial interview. "What tremendous ideas! What dreams! He's a genius, but is he all right in the head?" When Denis, Duc de Decrès, one of Napoleon's admirals, was asked if the Emperor would make a Russian city his capital, he replied bitterly, "He will not long have any capital; he will not return from this war; or if he returns, it will be without his army." Those around Napoleon noticed that his razor-sharp judgment seemed strangely blunted. His health, too, had deteriorated. He had become very fat and had perpetual stomach pains.

Napoleon at Saint-Cloud in 1812.

Still, his heart was set on Russia. "These barbarians," he said, "must be driven back into their own ice, so that for the next 25 years they won't come and interfere with civilized Europe." Despite having an army of 450,000 men, he planned an operation that would only have been practicable in a smaller country with a smaller force. They crossed the river Niemen, which formed the boundary between Prussia and Russia, on 24th June 1812. That day, a hare suddenly darted up between the legs of Napoleon's horse, causing it to swerve and throw him. He tried to laugh it off, but his touchiness showed that, like everyone else, he recognized it as a bad omen.

Men and horses were soon very short of food. It is now believed that about three quarters of Napoleon's army died, some in battle but most of starvation, before they even saw Moscow. The 800 kilometre journey to the capital began to seem an impossible task. They pressed on, the Emperor vaguely hoping for an opportunity to face the much smaller Russian army in battle, smash them and bring the campaign to a swift conclusion. But the Russians were not so foolish. As the Tsar had written a year earlier, "The system which has made Wellington victorious [in Spain], and exhausted the French armies, is what I am resolved to follow – avoid pitched battles. . ." The Tsar's ambassador in London foresaw events with incredible precision: "We can win by persistent defence and retreat. If the enemy begins to pursue us, it is all up with him; for the further he advances from his bases of supply and munitions into a trackless and foodless country, starved and encircled by an army of Cossacks, his position will become more and more dangerous; and he will end by being destroyed by the winter, which has always been our most faithful ally."

The march to Moscow took almost three months. It was only at the very end that the French caught up with the Russians outside Moscow, at Borodino, where they had dug themselves in. Napoleon's army was now reduced to half its number, and it had not yet fought a battle. Its task was made more difficult by the position of the Russian army, beside the Moskva river, on high ground with its centre protected by a formidable display of artillery. Napoleon knew his losses would be heavy. In the battle, which began on 7th September 1812, 600 French and 600 Russian guns pounded each other all day; 30,000 French and 44,000 Russians died. Both armies were broken, but, since it was the Russians who retreated, Napoleon could claim it as a

A patriotic print of Napoleon leading the French army into Moscow. In fact, the fire came during the night after they had occupied the city.

victory. Years later, however, he recalled it as "the most terrible of all my battles. . . . The French showed themselves worthy of victory, and the Russians worthy of being invincible." That mighty deadlock was itself an achievement of which the Russians could justifiably be proud.

But the way to Moscow was open, and a week later Napoleon entered it with the 130,000 soldiers who survived. To their amazement, they found the city totally deserted and silent. The entire population had abandoned it to the invaders. Undeterred, Napoleon occupied the Tsar's apartments in the Kremlin. But that night, one of his valets awoke in the small hours, to find that a glow in the sky was lighting up his bedroom. He looked out of the window, and saw that he was in the middle of a burning city.

The Russians had started fires throughout the city, after first immobilizing the fire engines. An incendiary fuse was even found in the imperial bedroom of the Kremlin. Strong winds made it impossible to prevent the fire from spreading. The stables, housing some of Napoleon's own horses, were saved by men working, as an eyewitness put it, "beneath a vault of fire". But whole districts of the city were completely destroyed.

After the fire was finally extinguished, the French stayed two weeks, while Napoleon waited for the Tsar to make

The burning of Moscow.

peace. But no message came. Napoleon could not understand it. He could have forced the Tsar's hand by marching on St. Petersburg, but the problems of maintaining discipline and preventing desertion on such a long trek were enough to deter him. So the French waited at Moscow, for a month in all.

That month turned out to be crucial. Typically, Napoleon was so convinced that the Tsar had to come to terms that he never considered what the consequences would be if he did not. He never thought of the Russian winter and scornfully dismissed the warnings of his aide, General de Caulaincourt, that a retreat in November and December could have terrible consequences. The weather itself, which remained mild long after autumn should have begun, helped to lull him into a false sense of security. Finally, a little snow fell, then a good deal of rain. Napoleon decided to abandon Moscow and retrace his steps a little way, in the hope of meeting and annihilating the Russian army and replenishing stores from stocks at Smolensk, which might well be the best place to spend the winter. (The route went past Borodino, where the corpses of the victims, still there after seven weeks, presented a grisly spectacle.) At Smolensk, which they reached on 9th November, came the appalling realization that the stores were far too depleted to be of much use. The starving men grabbed what there was. It was clear

Field Marshal Kutuzov, who had been a soldier for over fifty years when he commanded the Russian army against Napoleon in 1812. He died the following year.

that they would have to push on. Now winter began to set in. "It seemed as if the Emperor were expecting some miracle to alter the climate," noted de Caulaincourt. The horses, which were not shod for travelling on ice (de Caulaincourt, without telling Napoleon, had done that for the imperial household horses and so ensured their survival), fell and were left to die, or were cut up for food while they were still alive. Again, men began to die of starvation, and the news that Minsk, which might have provided stores, had fallen into Russian hands was a terrible blow. Boots wore out, exposing bare feet to frostbite. Soon, Napoleon's men were dying of cold, but still they did not forget to spare some firewood, when they had any, to warm their beloved Emperor. He, meanwhile, was looked after well, riding in a carriage drawn by his properly shod horses and provided with good meat and bread, his favourite vegetables (beans and lentils), and his favourite kind of Burgundy wine.

Gradually the great army was whittled away to almost nothing, but they had to march on, without food or adequate clothing, and if they died, they died. The stragglers and the wounded who were too weak to walk were an easy prey to marauding bands of Russians. Those that lived sometimes ate the corpses of their comrades. Many yielded to a craving for sleep and froze to death as they slept.

Napoleon's energy was undiminished. But, in the long days of the retreat, he had too much time for brooding, letting his imagination run on what might be going on at home. News reached him that, in Paris, a republican general called Claude François de Malet had tried to seize power in his absence. He decided to make a dash for home. There was no point in staying with the army, which was already destroyed. Only 4,000 men – out of over 450,000 – came back alive. Or, to put it as Napoleon did to the Senate in Paris: "My army has had some losses."

On 6th December, he and de Caulaincourt set out in haste for Paris. On the long, uncomfortable journey, part of it in a covered sleigh, Napoleon chattered endlessly of his future plans, boasting of his love affairs, complaining about the people who had the unenviable task of carrying out his orders. He belittled Wellington's success in Spain, saying "It cannot have any real importance, as I can change the

A contemporary watercolour of the French army's retreat from Moscow.

face of affairs when I please." They travelled around the clock, occasionally pausing for a meal or a brief rest. At Posen, in Prussia, Napoleon was delighted to receive affectionate letters from Marie-Louise. Finally, on 18th December, they reached their destination, so bedraggled that the porter of the Tuileries did not recognize them.

Defeat at Leipzig   Napoleon was back. The plot had been put down, but he faced another formidable problem. Prussia and Russia were re-arming, and he had no army. Half his fighting men lay dead in Russia; the others were tied up fighting Wellington in Spain. For years Napoleon had never considered the need to conserve the lives of his men, while Wellington never forgot it. Now was the moment of reckoning. Napoleon knew it. He said, "I sacrificed hundreds of thousands of men in Spain to keep my brother Joseph King." Someone with a spark of human feeling might have said, "Hundreds of thousands of men sacrificed *themselves* to keep my brother King." After the terrible slaughter at Eylau in 1807, he walked around the battlefield, turning over the bodies of his soldiers with his foot and muttering, "Small change." Now he was bankrupt.

Napoleon had always spoken of the "army of 1812", or of whatever year, as though it were a harvest whose crops could be eaten in the knowledge that there would be another harvest next year. He also once said that he had an annual "income" of 100,000 men. But, at the end of 1812, he was already training the following year's recruits, and, when they were ready, he immediately went on to those of the year after and the year after that. By 1813, his army was woefully inexperienced (though the one that replaced it in 1814 was even worse, consisting largely of youngsters who barely knew how to fire a musket). Against him stood Austria, Prussia, Russia and even Sweden (Bernadotte had changed sides).

The great confrontation, a battle lasting three days, came to Leipzig in October 1813. Napoleon, faced by an Allied army twice as big as his own, delayed his retreat until it was too late. The town's only bridge was blown up while the French were crossing. Napoleon and the Old Guard his special reserve troops were safely across, but the others were either killed in the fighting or drowned. The French marshals were torn between terrible grief and wild anger. "Would you like to review my army?" said one to his Emperor. "It won't take long. There's myself – I'm here already – and General Grundler, who'll be here in a minute."

53

The French being pursued through Leipzig on the last day of the battle, 19th October 1813.

Napoleon refused to make peace. The Allies, who had at first offered generous peace terms, withdrew them. For all his foolhardiness in continuing to fight, Napoleon's performance as a general in 1814 was superb. Wellington maintained that this year gave "a greater idea of his genius than any other." All his old audacity and mental agility returned and were matched by his army's incredible feats of valour, speed and its endurance of hunger and of murderous weather conditions. But their numbers were small. On 23rd March, a copy of the Emperor's orders fell into the hands of the Allies, and they decided simply to march on Paris and ignore Napoleon.

They arrived on 31st March and were instantly welcomed by Talleyrand as the representative of the newly formed Council of Regency, which had been formed to govern France until a new Head of State could be chosen. Talleyrand was most influential in deciding who that should be. There were a number of possibilities: the crown could be offered to Napoleon's brother Joseph, or to his little son, the King of Rome, or to Louis XVIII, the brother of the guillotined Louis XVI, who was still in exile in England. Talleyrand's moment of revenge on Napoleon had arrived. He persuaded the English that the Bonapartes were not to be trusted and that Louis XVIII should be crowned King of France.

Louis XVIII.

The return of Louis XVIII to Paris on 8th July 1815, after Napoleon's final defeat.

Napoleon arrived at Fontainebleau, outside Paris, to find that his capital city was in the hands of his enemies and that his wife and son had already fled. He talked wildly of further resistance until his marshals informed him bluntly that they would not obey him. He was obliged to abdicate on 6th April 1814.

7. Return

Napoleon never reached Paris. He stayed at Fontainebleau, where he had abdicated, and signed a treaty with the Allies. He and Marie-Louise were allowed to keep their titles as Emperor and Empress, in return for agreeing to leave France. It was the Tsar of Russia who suggested they should go to the island of Elba, between the coast of Italy and Corsica. Napoleon could have it as his own and trouble the world no longer. He was expected to take his wife and son, but they had gone back to Marie-Louise's parents in Vienna.

Napoleon was a broken man. One night he tried to commit suicide, but the poison was old, (it had accompanied him on the retreat from Moscow), and did not work. Before he left for his new home, he bade a tearful goodbye to his

Napoleon after his abdication, a painting by Paul Delaroche.

Napoleon departs for exile on Elba, 20th April 1814.

Old Guard in the courtyard of Fontainebleau Palace, which is still known as the "Court of Farewells".

He reached Elba after a journey through France during which he was made aware of his unpopularity. Often he was greeted with the cry "Down with the butcher of our children!" He quickly established an imperial court on Elba, at which his sister Pauline appeared out of sheer affection. He furnished his palace sumptuously, as though for a long stay, and took as much interest in governing Elba as he had in governing Egypt in 1798 or France thereafter.

Yet there were warning signs. He was constantly talking of war and recalling his old battles. He knew how unpopular the condescending Louis XVIII had made himself in France after only a few months. Though he was allowed only 400 of the Old Guard with him, he actually had 700. His mother exclaimed theatrically, "Heaven will not allow you to die by poison, or in your bed, which would be unworthy of you, but sword in hand!" To make it quite clear, she added, "Go forth and fulfil your destiny. You were not meant to die on this island." His old minister Maret sent a message suggesting that he should return to France. Quietly, Napoleon made plans to do just that.

A little fleet of seven ships was prepared and stocked. On the moonlit night of 26th February 1815, Napoleon and a thousand men boarded them and slipped away. Within three days, they had eluded the British and French ships and landed in the south of France. Now everything depended on how the French actually received him, and Napoleon knew it. Never in his life was he more charming or more inspired. He gave the performance of his career. Once, he found himself facing a detachment of the King's army, and simply walked towards them alone, saying "Here I am, don't you recognize me? If you want to kill your Emperor, all you need to do is fire." After a moment's stupefaction, they mobbed him ecstatically and shouted, "Long live the Emperor!" At Grenoble, people kissed his hands and garments, tore up the city gates and carried them to his hotel, crying "We could not offer you the keys, but here are the gates." Only rarely was there a moment of unease: at Cannes, a butcher tried to kill him. Less seriously, one innkeeper on the route flatly refused to cry "Long live the Emperor!" but, when genially requested by Napoleon to drink his health, he agreed.

Louis XVIII evacuated his capital city, accompanied by most of his ministers, and Paris prepared to change her loyalties once again. Napoleon was given a splendid reception. Cheering crowds in the Tuileries must have convinced him that he had nothing to fear. The enemy was the rest of Europe – Britain, Austria, Russia and Prussia, who were in conference in Vienna. Napoleon wrote to Talleyrand, trying to tempt him back, but Talleyrand contemptuously took the letter straight to the Austrian Emperor. He also made quite sure that Marie-Louise and the King of Rome did not go running back to Napoleon, as so many of his former generals had done.

Waterloo

War could not be long delayed. The Allied armies were still just on the far side of the Belgian border. Moreover, Napoleon's desire for a swift, dazzling success suggested the idea of reconquering Belgium, which had been French since very early in the war and had only been lost in 1814.

Waterloo in Belgium was the scene of the decisive battle of a series that had begun two days earlier, on 16th June 1815, at Ligny and Quatre-Bras. The 16th was a successful day for Napoleon, with both the British and the Prussians repulsed and heavy losses on the Prussian side. Yet, on the 17th, Napoleon did not follow up his success. As he was exhausted, suffering from a number of ailments, he made a late start to the day. His action was disastrous. A detachment commanded by the Marquis de Grouchy was sent out, supposedly to pursue the Prussians – a curious breach of the Emperor's usual rule to concentrate forces before a major battle. Ironically, the Allies were concentrating theirs, and the Prussians, instead of being where Grouchy's corps had been sent after them, were preparing to unite with the British under Wellington. Assured of this assistance, Wellington determined to fight it out with the French on the following day, 18th June.

In the end, to use Wellington's own phrase, Waterloo was "a damned nice [close] thing". The Prussians did not arrive until late in the afternoon, by which time the British were very hard pressed. Napoleon kept saying "They're ours! I've got them!" He was further heartened by the belief that the Prussian reinforcements had largely been destroyed at Ligny two days earlier and would not now amount to much. Finally, he imagined that Grouchy would bring his 30,000 men back to Waterloo; but Grouchy was not informed in time, and, having been told off once too often, dared not think for himself. When a wild shout, led by Napoleon, announced that Grouchy had returned, it was a terrible mistake; the "reinforcements" were Prussian.

Napoleon at the battle of Waterloo. A detail from a painting by Sir William Allan which now hangs in Apsley House, which was Wellington's London home.

A contemporary British print celebrating the exploits of Wellington's troops at Waterloo.

The battle ended with two hours of heroic cavalry charges by the French at immense loss. When the Guard was finally sent in and got into difficulties, panic set in among the other French regiments, and a general cry of retreat went up. Wellington had saved his cavalry until now. They made their decisive entrance, advancing with Blücher's Prussians and slaughtering the scattered French. Napoleon, shattered, weeping like a child and having to be held in the saddle, just managed to escape.

St. Helena

"I think we've done for 'em this time," said Wellington the next day. In Paris, the Chamber of Deputies shared his view. They proclaimed themselves in charge, egged on by Napoleon's old minister Fouché, who was busy settling scores against his master just as Talleyrand had done. Apart, perhaps, from appealing to the people, there was nothing Napoleon could do. He abdicated for the second time on 22nd June, 1815.

Napoleon withdrew to Malmaison, the house where he had lived with Josephine, who had died a few years earlier. She had grown much plumper as age advanced, but was still graceful, and still the perfect hostess. A chill caught through dancing strenuously with the Tsar and then walking in a cool garden had hastened her death. Napoleon became very sentimental about her, recalling her beauty and grace and thinking only of the love he had once felt for her. "Nothing ever came between us except her debts," he mused, forgetting the day he had sadistically ordered her carriage across the gully, or sat at the window of this very house, shooting her swans for fun.

He wanted to go to America and started reading books about it. Hoping for a safe conduct, he wrote an immensely grand letter to the Prince Regent of Britain asking for "protection" by "the most powerful, most constant and most generous of my enemies." Maybe, he thought, he could even go to England, living as a country gentleman and sending little Napoleon to acquire an upper class English education at Eton. But George III's ministers knew too well the power of Napoleon's charm. When he was kept for a few days on a British ship, the *Bellerophon*, which took him to Plymouth harbour to await the Government's decision, he had the officers and crew eating out of his hand. One said, "If the people of England knew him as well as we do, they would not hurt a hair of his head."

But, Britain was taking no chances. A few days later, Napoleon (addressed stiffly as "General Bonaparte") was horrified to learn that he was being sent to St. Helena, a tiny island in the middle of the South Atlantic, over a thousand miles from the west coast of Africa and even further from South America.

Napoleon embarking on the British ship *Bellerophon*.

Did he, even now, expect to escape? Possibly he expected to be recalled when a change of government, or of monarch, brought his friends to power in Britain. He was certainly charming throughout the nine weeks' voyage. He played cards and chess with the officers, and one of them sketched him. He had plenty of snuff, although he could no longer take other people's boxes as well. He only showed weakness once. At the last sight of France, he remained on deck for five hours, gazing at the retreating shore through a telescope. When it could be seen no more, he staggered back to his cabin, overcome with emotion.

The ship reached St. Helena on 17th October 1815. Napoleon said he didn't like the look of the place, and added: "I should have done better to stay in Egypt. I would be Emperor of all the East by now." Nevertheless, it was a beautiful tropical island, although rugged and rather small.

The worst of it from Napoleon's point of view was that he was not king here, as he had been on Elba. He was an honoured guest who did not have the option of leaving. Dozens of sentries were posted around his house. Apart from that he could do what he liked: talk, walk, read, supervise the gardening or have baths lasting for hours. He was even permitted to maintain something like royal protocol. Dinners were served formally, and his aides were obliged to stand for hours in his presence until they were practically dropping with fatigue. The house, Longwood,

A fanciful view of St. Helena in a contemporary French print.

was not palatial; it was a wooden building packed with grand furniture and infested to an almost incredible degree with rats, one of which surprised the Emperor by leaping out of his hat when he picked it up off the sideboard.

He was extremely well fed. He had more wine, particularly champagne, than he could drink, and kept a fancy pastrycook, who loved making the most breathtaking spun-sugar palaces and triumphal arches, "that looked as if they had been built for the Queen of the Fairies after her majesty's own designs". But the one luxury he wanted, he lacked: he could not leave. He could not even send and receive letters freely. In his frustration, he often became bad-tempered and vindictive. The Governor of St. Helena, Sir Hudson Lowe, a rather stolid man who was understandably determined to keep a close eye on his guest, had a terrible time with him.

Napoleon did make some friends among the English population, particularly with the Balcombe family, with whom he stayed for a few weeks while Longwood was being redecorated. There were two teenage daughters, the younger

63

Napoleon and the Balcombe sisters on St. Helena, as visualized in a French lithograph of the period.

of whom, Betsy, was golden-haired, blue-eyed, pretty and full of personality. Napoleon took to her instantly. She wrote that he was "almost boyish in his love of mirth and glee", but even then could not help sometimes seeing in it "a tinge of malice". She was a bit like that herself, taking pleasure in threatening him with his own sword, making him burn his hand with hot sealing wax, or simply inducing an English admiral's Newfoundland dog to bathe in the pond and then shake itself all over him. Nor was she distressed when the erstwhile Emperor was attacked by a cow, or when he jumped over a fence and landed in a cactus bush. But there were times when he was immensely kind. He loaded her and her sister with presents; once, when she was very ill, he made a point of enquiring regularly after her, and sent her all the kinds of sweets she liked. By the time the Balcombe family left the island in 1818, Betsy was a beautiful girl of sixteen, whose fondness and sympathy for Napoleon were those of a grown-up. They were very sorry to part.

Napoleon had mellowed a good deal. His aides constantly quarrelled amongst themselves, but he had become on the whole very patient. Only when they wanted to complain about what they saw as the inhumanity of confinement did he encourage them. Though these reports were exaggerated, the outside world mostly believed them. There was even an episode when the Pope, nobly forgetting his own rough treatment at the Emperor's hands, wrote a moving letter to the British Prince Regent, deploring Napoleon's "suffering" in captivity.

The worst form of suffering was boredom. There is a famous page in the diary of Gourgaud, one of Napoleon's companions, which reads: "Tuesday 25th: Boredom, boredom! Wednesday 26th: same. Thursday 27th: same. Friday 28th: same. Sunday 30th: Immense boredom." Napoleon talked about the past. He poured out his hatred for the treacherous British. Most of all, he justified himself and everything he had ever done. Loyally, his entourage listened, and those who were keeping diaries wrote down what he said. "If the Russians had not burned Moscow, I would have been Master of Russia. . . . I ought to have died at Moscow . . . or at Waterloo? If I had had Bessières or Lannes to command the Guard at Waterloo, I would never have been defeated. . . . I felt too confident of beating them. . . . I ought to have waited another fortnight. Perhaps I was wrong in attacking. . . ." And so on. One morning he said to Gourgaud, "Let it all end now. Don't you realize the bad moments I have when I lie awake at night, when I think of what I was, and what I am now?"

For years he had had a gastric ulcer. Now he developed cancer of the stomach, the disease that had killed his father and was eventually to kill his sister Caroline. He may also have had inflammation of the liver. In April 1821 he had a succession of fainting fits and vomitings. He became very weak and received the last rites of the Church. Early on 5th May, he spoke of Josephine, then of "the little King", then said, very distinctly, "At the head of the army. . ." Whether he was thinking of past successes, or of future hopes, nobody knew. After that, he spoke no more; only a tear or two trickled down his cheek in silence.

Napoleon on St. Helena.

He died that evening, after a tremendous storm that uprooted the saplings he had planted and blew down the old tree under which he loved to sit. When the first report of his death reached a distinguished gathering in Paris some weeks later, one of his former subjects spoke his epitaph: "Napoleon dead! What an event!" Inevitably, it was Talleyrand who murmured: "It is not an event. It is only news." Dressed in his uniform, as peaceful as a man asleep and as handsome as he had been twenty years before, the former Emperor was laid in a coffin that bore no name. Sir Hudson Lowe would not allow plain "Napoleon", as it seemed too imperial, and Napoleon's staff would not consider "General Bonaparte". Laid a few days later in a grave overhung by weeping willows, he remained there for nineteen years until his body was finally brought back to France.

Napoleon's career was brilliant, and his personality formidable. He was the greatest European statesman of his time, with a powerful vision of order and rationalization in society and the world. He was a great general and a great hero – but he was a hero flawed by arrogance, contempt for human life, and, most of all, by an insatiable greed for power. The Revolution had led only to Napoleon's imperial rule. After the slaughter of a king and millions of his subjects, another King, Louis XVIII, was back on the throne. As Marshal Foch, a great commander in World War I, wrote on the centenary of Napoleon's death: "He forgot that a man cannot be God; that, above man, there is moral law; and that war is not the highest goal, since above War is Peace."

Napoleon on his deathbed.

Chronology

This list of dates gives the main events in the life of Napoleon together with some of the many other things that were happening in the world at the time and are not mentioned elsewhere in this book. Events in bold type are covered in the main text of the book.

1769 **Napoleone Buonaparte born at Ajaccio, Corsica.**
1773 Boston Tea Party in protest against tea duty.
1774 Death of Louis XV; accession of Louis XVI. First Continental Congress of thirteen American colonies in Philadelphia. Joseph Priestley discovers oxygen.
1775 Start of War of American Independence. James Watt forms partnership with Matthew Boulton to manufacture Watt's steam engine.
1776 American Declaration of Independence. Publication of Adam Smith's *Wealth of Nations* and first volume of Edward Gibbon's *Decline and Fall of the Roman Empire*.
1778 United States and France form alliance against Britain.
1779 **Napoleon goes to Royal Military School at Brienne.** Spain declares war on Britain.
1780 Gordon Riots against Roman Catholics in London.
1781 British surrender to Americans at Yorktown. Ratification by states of US constitution completed.
1783 British recognize American independence in Treaty of Versailles. Montgolfier brothers make first ascent in fire balloon.
1784 **Napoleon leaves Brienne and goes to École Militaire in Paris.**
1785 **Napoleon graduates from École Militaire. Death of Carlo Buonaparte.**
1786 **Napoleon posted to Valence-sur-Rhône.** Death of Frederick the Great of Prussia.
1787 John Fitch launches steamboat on the Delaware River. Mozart's opera *Don Giovanni*.
1788 George III's first illness leads to Regency crisis in Britain. Mozart's *Symphonies Nos. 39–41*.
1789 National Assembly formed in Paris. **Fall of the Bastille. French peasant uprisings: the Great Fear.** George Washington elected first President of USA. Gilbert White's *Natural History of Selborne*.
1791 **French royal family attempt to escape from France.** Constitution makes France a constitutional monarchy. Mozart's opera *The Magic Flute*. James Boswell's *Life of Johnson*.
1792 **France declares war on Austria and Prussia. France proclaimed a republic.**
1793 **Execution of Louis XVI.** France declares war on Britain and Holland. **British occupy Toulon; Napoleon's part in its recapture wins him rank of Brigadier General.**
1794 **Execution of Augustin Robespierre ends The Terror in France.**
1795 **Start of Directory. Insurrection in Paris put down by troops under Napoleon.**
1796 **Napoleon marries Josephine. Italian campaign: Napoleon leads French victories against Austrians at Lodi, Arcole.**
1797 **Napoleon's triumphant return to Paris.**

1798 **Napoleon leads Egyptian campaign; victory in the battle of the Pyramids. French fleet destroyed by Nelson in battle of the Nile.** Thomas Malthus's *Essay on the Principle of Population*.
1799 **Napoleon returns to France.** *Coup d'état de Brumaire* **established the Consulate.**
1800 **French victory against Austrians at Marengo. France divided into administrative *départements*.** William Herschel discovers infra-red rays. Alessandro Volta makes first electric cell.
1801 Union of England and Ireland comes into force. Peace of Lunéville between France and Austria.
1802 **Napoleon becomes President of Italian Republic, and France annexes Italian states of Parma, Piedmont and Piacenza. Peace of Amiens between France and Britain.**
1803 **Britain declares war on France.** USA purchases Louisiana from France.
1804 **Bourbon plot. Execution of Duc d'Enghien. Napoleon crowns himself Emperor.**
1805 **British defeat French navy at Trafalgar. French military victories against Austrians at Ulm and Austerlitz.** Ludwig van Beethoven's opera *Fidelio* and *Piano Concerto No. 4*.
1806 **French defeat Prussians at Jena.**
1807 **Battles of Eylau and Friedland between French and Russians. Treaty of Tilsit.**
1808 **Establishment of the Imperial University. France invades Spain. British expedition to Portugal. Peninsular War.** Beethoven's *Symphonies Nos. 5 and 6 (The Pastoral)*. First part of J. W. Goethe's *Faust*.
1809 Battle of Corunna, Spain, between Britain and France. **Pope excommunicates Napoleon; Napoleon imprisons Pope. British successes in Peninsular War. French occupy Vienna. Napoleon divorces Josephine.** Chevalier de Lamarck publishes his evolutionary theories in *Philosophie Zoologique*.
1810 **Napoleon marries Marie Louise of Austria.** Charles XIII of Sweden names Bernadotte as his heir. France annexes Holland.
1811 **Birth of King of Rome.** Wellington drives French out of Portugal. Avogadro's hypothesis that gases are composed of molecules.
1812 **French invade Russia. Battle of Borodino. Occupation of Moscow and French retreat.** United States declares war on Britain.
1813 **Battle of Leipzig (Battle of the Nations).**
1814 **Allied armies enter Paris. Napoleon abdicates and is exiled to Elba. Accession of Louis XVIII.** British burn Washington, D.C. War between Britain and USA ended by Treaty of Ghent.
1815 **Napoleon escapes from Elba and is finally defeated at Waterloo; abdicates and is exiled to St. Helena.**
1818 **Balcombe family leave St. Helena.** Walter Scott's novels *The Heart of Midlothian* and *Rob Roy*.
1819 USA obtains Florida in treaty with Spain.
1820 Missouri Compromise over slavery in USA. Prince Regent becomes George IV on death of George III.
1821 **Death of Napoleon.** Start of Greek war of independence.

Books to Read

This list includes some of the many books in which you can read more about Napoleon and his times. Some of them are short and very readable, while others are large and detailed books that you may want to look at in libraries. The names of the British and American publishers and the date of first publication are given after each title. Many of the books have also been published in paperback.

NAPOLEON

Napoleon David Chandler (Weidenfeld & Nicolson/Macmillan Inc., 1973)
Napoleon: Master of Europe 1805-1807 Alistair Horne (Weidenfeld & Nicolson/William Meyer, 1979)
Napoleon and his Parliaments 1800-1815 Irene Collins (Edward Arnold/St Martin's Press, 1979)
The Military Life of Napoleon Trevor Nevitt Dupuy (Franklin Watts, 1969)
'A Near Run Thing', The Battle of Waterloo David Howarth (Collins/Atheneum, 1968)
The Battle of Waterloo Jackdaw folder (Cape/Viking)
The Retreat from Moscow Jackdaw folder (Cape/Viking)
Josephine & Napoleon Margaret Laing (Sidgwick & Jackson/Mason Charter, 1973)
Napoleon's Second Empress Patrick Turnbull (Michael Joseph/Walker, 1971)

CONTEMPORARIES

Nelson Roy Hattersley (Weidenfeld & Nicolson/Saturday Review Press, 1974)
Nelson and his World Tom Pocock (Thames & Hudson/Viking, 1968)
Robespierre: the Force of Circumstances John Laurence Carr (Constable/St Martin's Press, 1972)
Wellington: The Years of the Sword Elizabeth Longford (Weidenfeld & Nicolson/Harper & Row, 1969)

FRENCH REVOLUTION

The French Revolution Christopher Hibbert (Allen Lane/William Morrow, 1980)
The First European Revolution 1776-1815 Norman Hampson (Thames & Hudson/W. W. Norton, 1969)
Life in Revolutionary France G. Lewis (European Life series, Batsford/Putnam, 1972)
A Social History of the French Revolution Norman Hampson (Routledge & Kegan Paul/University of Toronto Press, 1963)
A History of Modern France Vol. II: 1799-1871 Alfred Cobban (Penguin, 1957)

Index